21 PARTICLES OF ETERNITY

ARCHIVE ZERO | NEW YORK | 2019
www.archivezero.com

Published by Archive Zero, LLC

E-book ISBN: 978-0-9975442-4-4
Paperback ISBN: 978-0-9975442-5-1

Cover design by Robson Garcia Jr.
Cover photo: Kelvin C. Bias
(near Vik, Iceland, Oct. 21, 2012)
Formatting by Polgarus Studio

"If everyone in every country had a friend in every other country, the prospects for war, hate, poverty, climate inaction, famine, and a host of other world problems, would approach zero. Let's approach zero together."

Kelvin C. Bias, Publisher

for my daughters

Contents

21 PARTICLES OF ETERNITY

21 PARTICLES OF ETERNITY

Every now and then I catch a glimpse.
A shrill sound. A crack of light.
A moan against the delirious night.
When worlds fall away and
Reunite. Twilight:
The usual entryway.
Perchance the best.
Therein lies the conundrum,
The carnal emporium.
One, you are there.
Twenty more with care.
The door remains unlocked
As we bend on the linoleum floor.
1970: 1,970.
Time and again.
They see tomorrow then.
We see them tomorrow.
Glide past the hatred.
Remain satiated in the chains of love.
The bonds broken to express freely.
With another, with the other,
With the shard of the pleasure lover.
Attain nirvana. Whisper as you wonder.
I salute your body.

Listen to my words.
The poetry is within you.
You make the nations sing.
You bake the peace.
Look under the sofa.
Everything is there.
Kept lovers to yourself.
Kept ecstasy shared with
One another. Smothered.
I always want you this way.
21 particles of eternity:
How many more will we find?

WE ARE THE MARTIANS

Richat, Richat.
The eye of the Sahara
Is upon us. Bullseye.
Target acquired.
Spinning, pressure, heat.
Quartzite residue.
The water planet.
The water we desperately need.
The water we are made of.
Life, the product. DNA.
Sprung forth of necessity.
Of tempered energy.
Of hopes and eons.
We are the Martians.

ICELAND

Black sand, blue sky.
Basalt reaching high.
Reynisdrangar stands guard.
The blonde whirl of a
Danish tourist.
A photographer eyes
A volcanic flame.
Vík. The succulent dawn.
The North Atlantic licking
The lap of ecstasy in a
Roadside sanctuary.
Two lovers hoping to find
Passion in unknown regions:
Viceland.
Clouds recede and
Selnafoss deafens.
As a gravel road
Leads to nowhere.

LOS ANGELES

The space of the grid.
Nothing misunderstood.
The Milky Way reflected,
Mulholland's horizon.
Top-of-the-line. Sublime.
Waves breaking,
Starlets bloodletting.
We watch the dream.
On the big screen.
Pay our fee. Happily.
Waiting for a Hollywood sign.
Dawn, dusk and LAX
Abandoned streets
Interrupted by a lone soul.
Lining up his shot on
A skateboard.
There is no ice.
Traffic stands still.
Sepulveda, PCH, PCP.
We smile, we flee.
Then turn up the sun.
And do it all again.

A DARK MAN WITH
A DARK HAT

Many people think they know his name.
They run from him, while watching
From the shadows, corruption untold.
Stark light silhouettes the scene.
Black and white Tri-X.
16mm, Sweet 16, 16 minutes ago,
The lord of mischievousness
Descended, dandy and dignified.
Everyone already has an idea.
He doesn't blink.
He places a black fedora.
Atop his curly locks.
Clocks rewind in ladies' minds.
A regal delight. Corduroy and soul.
Sinister he is not.
Just a dark man in a dark hat,
Standing in a dark alley,
Trying to avoid the spotlight.

SEA OF INK

Open water.
Thoughts unborn.
Sun above, darkness below.
The words a shelter
From the raging blue.
The mind, unleveled.
Unsettled by stories,
Ideas, dreams,
Vast imaginings,
Targeted for the universe.
I need a constellation
In the infinite night.
A cure for insomnia.
It's always there.
A pound of flesh,
A pound of flexed
Fingers on an
Illuminated key.
Drowning, drowning
In a sea of ink.

DIVISION 21

Dress blues.
The war to end all wars.
My check didn't come in.
My arm is still attached
To the soil, somewhere
In a foreign land.
Gunnery wasn't so lucky.
His future stuck in the past.
On a roadside under
A damning sun.
I stand tall and salute
Through misty rain.
Listening to the echo
Of 21 Guns.

ALL THE DEAD THINGS

The sound of spring rain
In the aftermath of pain.
Songs sung, amplified.
Dignified, then petrified.
Memories thrown out
Discarded, a last shout.
The romance is gone.
Dissolved in the flick of a wand.
No sand, no beach, no carnal
Revival of a sanctified arsenal.
The remains far flung
The healing black lung.
Eventually they return.
They yell and burn.
The words muffled by the fire,
Crackling tinder, dire.
Clinking rings and
All the dead things.

TOMORROW'S BREAKFAST

Beyond the mundane.
Cellophane and tears.
A dream vanquished,
A line remembered from
A film you've seen ages past.
Nothing lasts yet we seek
The continued confusion,
The utter nonsense
Shaped into a beautiful
Sculpture, draped in death.
Gleaming for eternity.
These are lesser concerns
In the middle of the nightclub
Eyes wide and searching
For the next fix.
Tomorrow's breakfast.
When will it come?

5:11 A.M.

The birds are chirping,
Breaking dark's cold silence.
Sunrise is nigh.
Your sleeping breaths drawn
Under an ominous sky.
Orange haze tries to break through.
Enough, enough.
Let's commence Round X.
For the birds are chirping,
The birds are chirping.

WORDS ARE MY CANVAS

Words are my canvas.
They cause me to seek joy
In the beatitudes of life.
Beneath, on the surface,
And above still waters.
They chasten with haste,
They proclaim, they jest.
They brag, they sing,
They swirl in happiness.
They never hide.
They love you.
Words are my shelter.
I lie down in them.
I linger in their sound.
I exalt them.
I paint with their brush.
I remember their taste.
I don't need words
To define myself.
Yet hold them evermore, for,
Without words, the meaning
Of love is rendered moot.

METALLIC LOVE

She looked like a ghost
Stepped, and steeped,
Straight from the *Metropolis* poster.
Eyes wide in a hollow suit.
Hallowed in her beauty,
The city bends to
Her magnetic charm.
I fly, horizontal.
Unable to break free.
I don't want to flee.
I crave her inner cells.
My mercury boiled by
Her heat, her radiant orbs.
Her metallic attraction.
I am weak: never steeled.
I want to penetrate her
Spaceship and land
In an eternal future.
For I am metal too.

GOO

Little words,
Little mischievous smirks.
Little fingers latched
Around my heart:
The toddler two.
Faster, higher,
"I can do it myself."
From take off my shoe
To family hug time.
Enjoy your journey
Among the stars.
The heart attack twins.
Sunshine is your friend.
You can come out and play.
Your futures await.
Your excitement over
A dandelion supersedes
Everything, big and small.
Ice cream, you scream.
We all scream for the swings.
All Mom and Dad can do:
Stop and admire.
As you say "Okay".
For we are goo.

LITTLE JOYS

Sleeping angels in the
Other room.
In the darkness,
The quiet of night,
Tired from a day of
Discovering new ways
To climb a jungle gym,
And the window sill.
The questions rise
With each breath.
Imperceptible beneath
Tiny rib cages.
One follows the other.
"That's mine."
This, that and the other.
Sleep is their domain.
The guardian, Father,
Stands nearby, melted,
Looking, locked in time,
At his little joys.

ALONE ON A TRAIN
SOMEWHERE IN SPAIN

Naive.
Before Jillian and Anne.
Before the looped
Downfall.
And the…
I.
Don't.
Give.
A.
Fuck.
Phase.
A young man, solo.
On a European sojourn.
Pure.
Innocent.
Unsullied by heartbreak.
Possessing a wicked grin
That doesn't know its power.
Finland.
Germany.
Las Vegas.
Cannes.

Before O.J.
Before rings.
Before beautiful kids.
Back to New York,
New York.
Where the man
Remembers being
Alone in the rain
On a train.
Somewhere
In Spain.

THE SCULPTOR

Stand at the center
Of an all white room.
Bare against the tides
Of time and fear.
A quarry on the floor.
While you burn
Me with your stare.
Masquerade for eternity,
Cloaked in sensuous cries.
I aspire for more.
I desire your core.
I am a sculptor.
Seeing forever
In your lithe form.
I don't want or need
To touch a thing.
Though dearly
I wish I could
Reach out and feel.
I'll pick up a chisel:
Caelum. I will fail.
You are perfect.
Nothing I do would equate.
I smile wide and true.

Then turn to marble.
As a tear wells and
Runs down your nude form.
I'll pose for you instead.

VIDEO GIRL

The moment of flawless lust,
A word not patient enough.
More consonants, syllables,
To represent the earthly desires
Drawn out over hours, days, weeks.
Months later, still engorged.
Still letting go.
Glistening bodies in shining light.
Frozen. Lips pressed firm.
Showered with fervor.
Too busy to talk.
Legs too beautiful to mock.
Silhouetted by exacting form.
The line on your back, a groove,
A pathway to perilous pleasure.
Five minutes left,
The climax to attack.
Rest. Rewind. Refresh.
You're unstuck
In time. All mine.
Everyone's favorite girl.

RED'S DREAM

Red sat up in bed,
Sweaty, confused.
Unhinged by heartbreak,
Long ago, far afield:
A desert highway
Through monuments,
A Colorado plateau.
Day and date unknown.
The clouds were no help.
98 years young.
Time shrouded his will.
He remembered
Her black hair.
He couldn't remember
Her name.

A CLOUD WITH YOUR NAME

Legs intertwined.
Your skin, all mine.
The sky, a brethren in love.
Pink, light blue,
White and grey.
We unite beneath
A canopy of tomorrow.
Brows furrowed,
Eyes wide. Unison.
Distraction reigns.
While winds whip
Across our bodies.
Look up, remain
Affixed to the order
Of the heavens.
Together, clear,
We are divine.
Held dear by desire.
As I whisper
Gladly in your ear.
We are one.
We are forever.
As I exhale, I am
Destined to become
A cloud with your name.

THINGS I'VE DONE THAT
ADD UP TO NOTHING

Lamented. Exalted.
I allowed myself to forget
Before I remembered.
Some things I've done:
Walked *le tapis rouge*
In Cannes. Draped in dreams.
Kissed a girl in Hong Kong.
Divided and conquered none.
Wept in the dead of night
Upon the passing of my Dad.
Entered Carnegie Hall
Without practicing.
Vomited on the sidewalk,
Danced drunk and bled.
Watched aspirations rise,
disappear, and reappear.
Laughed when insincere.
Drank clear water in Japan.
Peered across the Grand Canyon,
Hoping its grooves outlived us.
Sank when my heart split.
Dislocated my left pinkie,

Stared crooked as we fled.
Scored a touchdown in
A scrimmage at the end
Of football practice
Beneath an Arizona sky.
Married in the neon graveyard
Of Las Vegas, waylaid.
Walked the Champs-Élysées,
The Champ du Mars,
Père Lachaise.
Witnessed the dawn on a
Galapagos Island.
Sauntered from the Mediterranean
After writing it all down
Under a moonlit night
In a Mallorcan windmill.
Rose in a cold sweat.
Died in my nightmare.
Awoke in a hot flash
Lying next to sin,
The ornaments of pleasure
Scattered about the room.
Failed miserably in many regards.
Succeeded in many others.
Milked a cow. A milkman cometh.
Sled down a snowy Norway path,
Vanished in Vigeland.
Rambled into a foggy bar
On 14th Street when I

Saw a gorgeous star.
Reminisced about "back in the day",
Reminded myself: That day is now.
Alighted on a jumbo jet.
Bound for World Cup glory.
Mexico 1, Germany 0.
The lights, the lights.
Defeated Russian nights.
Discovered *Playboy*,
Centerfolds and fantasy.
Sang a bad karaoke song.
Imagined I was the star
Killin' on the big screen.
Floated through the air
With the greatest of ease,
Unaware the world didn't care.
Sunrise haunted my thoughts.
Sunset delivered them back.
Sauntered on Santa Monica Pier.
Saw Lakers-Celtics Game 4 in 1984.
Rambis clotheslined.
Another loss, another year.
I climbed into the batter's box,
Swung in fear. Strike Three.
Forgot to take out the trash.
Signaled the wrong way
On an eerily desolate,
Two-lane desert highway.
Headed into oblivion,

Then made a U-turn.
Took off my clothes
And had ecstatic spins.
Sinned and grinned.
Never minded the result.
The past passed by.
And what remains?
A clown, wasted time now and then.
Smiled when I did it all again.
And it added up to nothing.

78 DEGREES AND SUNNY

What's the temperature of your sky?
The temporary reason for a fleeting
Condition is like bending the knee
Or dying, simply for the weather.
It will change whether or not you do.
Clouds billow, then fly away.
Winds whip through Laurel Canyon.
The wild fires wild in the hills.
Love flees then rekindles on another
Mountain or Hollywood bungalow.
June Gloom? Allay impending doom.
The sun is a constant friend.
When it erupts and engulfs us all,
You can rest easy in this notion:
Within the canopy of your imagination,
It's always 78 degrees and sunny.

A MILLION YEARS

Before the world is born,
Before the fire burns us all.
Before the fall of unicorns,
You and I embrace, stand tall.

We swirl, lost in the sea of time
We dance and don't rescind.
We fly, our naked bodies, entwined.
Together, faster than the wind.

Eons past we left the planet blue.
After the rain and precious tears,
If I made love to you,
I'd live a million years.

VORTEX

The dark clouds:
Wayward wizards.
Looking for a sorceress,
I am the warlock.
The cauldron of emotion,
Standing askew,
Society balanced on a hill.
You cannot do this.
You cannot do that.
Fantasies do not lie.
Until one day nigh,
The heavens part,
The rays refract infinity
And you appear
Through the open door.
Scandalous beauty,
Night engulfs us.

TOYS AND CUPCAKES

From the mind of a child.
A magnetic message
On the refrigerator.
A gracious appreciation
For favorite things
And the parental
Capacity to fulfill dreams.
"Thank you, Mommy,
For buying toys
And cupcakes."
All you need in life:
Destined desires and
Heartfelt gratitude.
A lesson from a 4-year old
Via cupcakes and toys.
Witnessed and held.
A monolithic note
From the sunlight zone.

GREEN STREETS

The city, pre-planned.
A testament to the strength
Of the human engine.
Powered without fossils.
Powered without waste.
Powered without death.
Wash the air with
Silky clouds of mist.
Rain falls and collects.
Tides ebb and flow,
Leading the energy glow.
Cars guide themselves.
People protect the world.
Everyone is a guardian
Amongst the infinite glass
Structures filled with trees.
CO_2 no more. Removed,
Refurbished, rebirth
Of the Earth.
This is our city.
The only one we know.
We ponder as we wander,
Hand in hand enthralled,
Admiring these green streets.

EVERYONE IS BEAUTIFUL

Everyone is beautiful.
Everyone is pain.
Everyone is strong.
Everyone is game.
Everyone is sad.
Everyone is slain.
Everyone is joyous.
Everyone is lame.
Everyone is beautiful.
They argue just the same.

EYES

A universe within.
Empties its soul
Into another.
A vine in time.
Seeing tomorrow,
Seeing yesterday,
Seeing nothing
More than the
Illusion of the
Physical reality
We think we create
When somebody
Else is watching.
We join.
We unwind.
We look into the
Furthest reaches
When the eyes
Are all we behold.

BLUE HORSES

There, below the sky,
Like a painter's tear
Amid the tumbling
Azure reflection in
A never-ending pool:
Stark creatures,
Stately in the sun.
Manes whipping
Locked in equine
Circles. Flying.
As they walk on
Water. Feet stomping
In time. Rhythm.
Only blue.
Tails batting the eyes
Of all who behold.
I am awestruck
By the stamped,
One color true.
I know the secret;
Your salacious visions
Are my wild horses.

PABLO IS BACK

A slogan writ large
On the side of a
Gentrified building.
It's not graffiti,
It's a declaration.
A lover? An enemy?
Pablo, a man unknown
To the passerby
With a stroller.
Two girls dangling,
Laughing into twilight.
A man, a father, a saint?
All three imagine.
Made up beliefs.
Withering but not
Forgotten. A statue.
A decadent dreamer.
He's back and
We're still here.

THE LAGOON

Somewhere on
The circle of time.
A coral vergence,
Where wind confuses
Direction. Inoculated
From the sands of escape.
A woman or a dream?
Dark hair unfurled
Against the enveloping
Sky. Life out of view.
Hours, minutes mean
Infinity in this paradise.
Flotsam, jetsam, a plan.
Dive into the center.
The lagoon. Heal,
Before memories
Kill your sun-baked mood.
1913 or the distant past.
Izumi, find me.
Find me true.
Find me beneath
The enduring blue.

AMBIENT

Whispers deep in the field.
Electric, succulent symposium.
Synthetic beats among
Pulsating hearts.
Amethyst crystal,
Piercing lights.
We weave in the throng.
The young, the strong.
Heeding the ambient call.
Fall may never come.

WHITE SHEETS

You are my cocoon
Versus the rising tide of hate.
A beautiful respite
From the dawn's color.
Let's fade away,
Together, unblind.
Only momentarily
As we embrace,
Then happily clean
The sheets.

A MILLION POEMS

One enduring kiss.
A flowering of love
In a cenotaph.
Eternal hands
Dreaming,
Wishing,
Remembering.
The words remain.
I'd be remiss
If I didn't tell you
Before it's too late.
I'll write a million poems
For your gracious lips.

LOVEMAKING BY DEATH

We heard a friend had died.
We made calls, inquiries,
Sat solemnly in the dark
In separate beds.
Quiet without
Appropriate tears.
Feelings torn,
Rendered worse
By the dual finality
Of goodbyes.
Farewell, to the living.
Maybe we'll make love
In the afterlife.

THE OTHER PLANET

How many light years away?
Before we forget our genesis.
Before we destroy another world.
Before we end it all.
In a Petri dish,
The cycle reborn,
Or your sphere is
Off limits to all life forms.
Distant DNA: cohesion.
Firmaments assigning
Elegance and alien contraband.
There is no one there.
There are many there.
Somewhere in between?
No matter. We must believe:
This *is* the other planet.

LEGS

You calm my restless mind.
Then create new quandaries
With your gamine seduction.
Blue jeans in a smoky room.
Bare feet dangling from
The edge of the pool table.
I could play for days.
Go on and on.
Never spilling a beer.
Until you walk past.
A beautiful distraction.
Eight ball, wrong pocket.
Damn you and your legs.

SPACE GIRL

Air locked, lips tight.
The perfect suit
800 million miles away,
Counting down,
Counting up.
Flickering stars beckon.
A roving mind
Entangled with
Orion's Belt.
When will you return?
One Earth soul.
One Earth lifetime.
Light years and matrimony.
I'll give you the
Rings of Saturn.

BEAUTY IS A SWORD

The paramount sign,
An appealing beacon,
A mirror reflecting the stars.
Within the shards,
You stand. Eternal.
Beholden to none.
Everyone looks.
Everyone cooks
Their own fantasy,
Forging steel and
Waging war for
Your attentions.
Strange gazes,
Stranger gifts.
You fight the throng
With grace and humility,
With manners and concern.
Your knowledge is
Your unbroken shield.
And beauty is a sword.

WE'RE ALL HUMAN HERE

32 floors with the bells on the doors
32 floors with the bells on the doors.
The ward full of watchers, waiters,
Seekers and charlatans.
Varlets imagined stirring their cauldron.
Visiting hours, dead morning flowers.
We sedate the young and kill the old.
No one's alert; no one's immune.
The nurses strapped in, mind out.
As we sing our great tune.
How did we get here?
We human, we three.
We dance like the others.
Why can't we go free?
White coats and white milk.
Medicine, they say.
Medicine for dreamers.
And the uneven cleaners.
Night after night.
Year after year.
Am I not human? Am I not here?
32 floors with the bells on the doors
32 floors with the bells on the doors.
We're all human here.

LINOLEUM

I drip for you.
Tomorrow, noon and night.
Blinded by your lucidity,
Your fierce devotion
To your powerful curves,
And their ability to
Make my blood rush
Like a volcanic river,
Swallowing everything
But the kitchen sink.
Do you scream my name
In the lonely hours
When no one hears?
Except the cold linoleum.
The barren space of
My heart needs to be filled,
To capture your essence,
To wipe the floor of my brain.
I listen in these dusty evenings.
Alone too in my own prison.
Let's dream simultaneously,
In the dark, an alluring pair.
Climax in perfect sync.
Glisten as one beast.

Then scamper gleefully
As we search for
The cleaning materials.

BLOOD

Chi, chi, chi.
Lifeforce infused.
Blood confused,
Amused. Remember.
Pump, flex and spoon.
Our bodies swoon.
Our symptoms elate.
Ecstasy is in your veins.
Lurking, a patented passenger.
We obey the simian call.
Delighting with fury.
In the middle of the city.
Words and worlds disappear.
Glistening sweat manifests
Beyond the heart.
Down to the bone.
Where we wallow
Amongst our souls.

FORGIVENESS

Things unspoken unravel
The best of times,
Creating the worst.
Rise above the din,
The abyss of revenge.
Let hatred fall in,
Never to return.
The weight of anger
Destroys from within.
Forget the pain,
Remember the diversion,
The happiness of lost
Shadows at sunset.
You won't regret.

MORNING DREAM

Eyes wide open,
A finger pointing
To the sky,
To the decision:
What to do today,
Where to go and sing.
Comfortable wings
Waiting to alight
In mother's arms,
On father's shoulders,
Holding sister's hand.
Awake, but still.
The air filled with
Coos and gesticulations.
Morning is the guide.

BLUE AXIS

We are not an army,
A marauding band
Of capitalistic scions.
We are lovers.
We are friends.
We are others,
Dancing free.
Looking backward
At a glorious sun:
The light of the world.
We are a blue republic.
A city on the edge of
Tomorrow, frequented.
Visited by war,
By peace, by silence,
By beautiful moments,
By shining children,
By difficult nothing.
When we join the tilt,
We spin together
On a life-giving axis.
We solve all the problems.
We end the discussion.

THE JOY OF
LIFTING A FINGER

Subtle sibilance.
Neurons captured and dispossessed.
Paused, an identity crisis.
Prone to great feats of mind,
An immobile magician waves his wand.
Every breath a gift, every dream a birth.
Walking takes a grant,
A willful connecting spirit.
Imagination surpasses atrophy.
Nurses change sheets.
Visitors smile while wishing
They could look away.
The prostrate penitent remembers.
Every stolen kiss, every spasm,
After the track meet in the 11th grade.
The free fall into the long jump pit.
The shriek of pain from a shattered hurdle.
They are memories, shafts of time,
Invisible to all. Scars deep, unseen.
Each day the recumbent
Reveals the same winking joke:
Bask in the joy of lifting a finger.

The action is the reward,
Your Mount Olympus.
The fire, unextinguished.

THE THIRD DEATH OF
ANNE VAN OOSTEN

Paris. London. Rome.
Flight attendant
To a bruised heart.
The protagonist in a
Splendid life.
A figment of
The imagination.
She exists somewhere.
We made love once.
Maybe thrice.
Long ago, languished
In excising arguments.
We loved love, making
The world seek shelter.
The girl on the side.
The man on her mind
As she masturbated at work.
Or so he was told.
Or so he believed.
Gone their separate ways:
The first death.
Years later, rekindled.

Tumbleweeds refined.
We were so inclined.
Meeting in hotel rooms
At curious hours.
Somewhere on 27th Street.
Filled with furious joy.
Until tomorrow ended,
We vowed not again,
This is the last time.
No more flights to miss.
The second death wrought
Silence. A final kiss.
Time passed. 365 days
Plus, a decade or more.
Middle-age dreams.
Shattered on the floor.
We bumped randomly
Into one another,
Bathed by an ominous sky,
One final rendezvous.
Dutch cobblestones.
Norwegian wood.
Hot chocolate awaited.
We agreed to meet
Two weeks hence.
Another flight, happenstance.
Vienna. For an eternal glance.
I took off my clothes;
The hours passed.

The sun set; the clock bled.
Then I heard the news.
Flight 99. All presumed dead.
I packed up. Cried.
There was nothing left.
The suit left hung
In the solemn closet.
I became a ghost. You,
A name on a tombstone.
I rose not quite as tall.
The third death of
Anne Van Oosten.
The worst of them all.

STARSHIP LOVE

The fate of our species
Breeds somewhere on
A generation ship
Beyond Vega.
Embryos programmed,
Waiting to be born,
Frothing in a sentient bath.
Flesh hung in perfect rows.
Bodies, minds, fantasies.
Driven by precision,
Of love and lust.
We forgo war. Reclaim dust.
Breath to breath
And breast to breast.
Starship Love is our new home.
Where fleeting aspirations
Continue in the continuum.
We warp past light speed,
Our souls attached to beams.
Colonizing eternity.

SILENCE

Frogs bellow in rice patty lairs.
Fog kisses mountain tops.
Electricity fortifies the air.
Dreams remain in place.
Beneath *Kawara* roofs,
The Land of the Rising Sun sleeps.
Peace alights over *sugi* wood heaven,
While babbling brooks break free.
Morning light is the ward of the valley.
Snakes slither, crickets chirp,
A hawk searches for breakfast.
The wind turns up the volume.
The sound of clouds extols life,
The crack of distant thunder.
Ajisai await the coming storm.
Before the sleeping angels awake,
Standing as silhouettes
Against a fertile dawn,
The waker listens.
Silence has no domain here.

MAGNANIMOUS TRUTH

Painful, but undrawn blood.
A knife in the light.
Words no truer told
Echo with the wind.
I move aside,
Inspecting my reaction.
Introspective. Serene.
Your action is my traction.
You know what to say.
I must listen.
Turn the wheel.
The superlative ears, destiny.
I have to grow to rise.
I have to rise above,
Soar higher than
The malaise.
Tell me again:
Get your shit together.

NAMIBIAN RIVER GOD

Acquired in a desert land
By a girl of beautiful persuasion.
The sphere of Walvis Bay.
Traversed far and away.
How she gained possession,
I'll never know.
I didn't ask, but nay,
I wouldn't tell anyway.
A bringer of rain or
A piece of someone's heart,
Out of which something grew.
A man destined to fade.
Bequeathed to me by her love.
A wooden hook wrapped
With glorious twine.
A symbol, a sign,
In time, a weapon of sadness,
Burning a hole in my pocket,
Slow burning anger
Through a brain's veins.
I couldn't bear it,
This hot piece of coal
In my jeans, weighing
Down my soul, my desires.

It wouldn't last, like
Sand through fingertips:
Namibian grains.
So I gave it back to the girl.

SAPIOSEXUAL

Your brain drives a tornado,
The whirlwind of thoughts,
Equations, gravity flipped.
I am caught in your field,
In your teaching eyes.
I see your magnificence multiplied,
A mind accompanied by
Beautiful symphonies.
Play my keyboard.
Fill me with your knowledge.
For I am electrified
In your presence,
In your all-seeing nakedness.
Bared inquisitiveness,
Curiosity, indulgence
For your lesser fiend.
I am fury in your intelligence.
I am stronger than our magnetic
Attraction. I am lust.
Thirsty for the power you possess.
Plug me into enlightenment.
And fill my memory bank.
Titillated by conscious desire,
I fall asleep in your head.

There, here, everywhere.
I want you, I want you.
I need your upgrade.

SUMMER SNOW

The chill in the room matches
Our frosty demeanor,
The sour milk, cold,
in a bare refrigerator.
Money isn't the issue,
It wafts in and out
Like the Freon-cooled air.
Our love, condensation,
Compensation for a grueling
Argument, transfixed on coils,
Conditioned and primed,
Frozen in time. We let it go.
I'll kiss you again, then,
When my tears turn into snow.

IF I DIE TOMORROW

If fate takes my soul,
Tomorrow on the hour,
Will there be a record,
An elegiac song, played,
Or thoughts rearranged?
Will my blood dry,
Become powder
For opportunistic maggots?
Will I know the day before?
Act according to a
Hedonistic plan.
Or walk in the park and
Talk to family, friends?
Will my living essence
Flow into the universe
Or into your good graces?
Will appeal still abound
Around the world?
Or will two lovers,
Grasp harder, kiss
And sweat passion?
The answers need not
Be fully unbound.
Let them be lost,

Gone to the arrow of time.
If I die tomorrow,
Let's make love today.

LOVING YOU

I expect no reward.
I get no receipts.
Just a bagful of groceries,
Picnics and treats.
There isn't a set schedule.
Monotony hasn't set in.
Pump the human organ.
Play the loudest notes.
Even if you don't
Acknowledge me.
Or require desirous more.
I'm here.
Loving you.
Down on the floor.

BLACK KING

Master of his domain,
The world unchained.
Unbridled, unbound.
The point of no return:
Adieu Gorée.
A statue alive.
Bronze and ebony.
A kingdom, no King down.
A man among men.
There are millions.
One king of many.
Nothing stands taller.
Locked arms. Power.
We stand free.

MISTER PARADISE

I can stand you up,
Set you free.
Make you
Yell from the
Mountaintop,
Endlessly.
I'm a man,
A dreamer who's free.
Don't worry about
Tomorrow. It inches
Eventually.
I'm Mister Paradise.
I'll make you some tea.

WHY?

Why does rain fall from the sky?
A million questions with
A twinkle in their eyes.
Two daughters giggle
On my weakened knees.
Why is water wet and
Ice so cold?
I ponder the answers
Then listen some more.
As one grabs my ear
And another jumps
On my head,
I can't leave their
Curiosity in the
Land of Untold.
Why do we dream
When we fall fast asleep?
Why don't cars stop
At the traffic light?
For these and much
More. Stay here with me.
In this moment, don't age.
A tear plops on my cheek.
And two little voices peak:
Why, Daddy, why?

TINY FINGERS

Born of love.
Wonders from above.
Eyes flutter open,
A locked stare
Defines a lifetime.
Minds in time,
Growing together.
Electric happiness
Transferred by touch.
I want to hold your
Tiny fingers until
They grow up.

THE LAST ICEBERG

Atop the Arctic lee.
Below the Antarctic sea.
Two distant lovers melt,
Calving to be together.
They know their destiny.
They drift, they dream.
First one, down to a tip.
The northern warrior.
Settled, resigned, calm.
A blip and he's gone.
While his female counterpart
Remains afloat, astute.
Constituted by frozen desire.
Blue within blue.
White shelves beckon.
As a tern relays the message,
Before all is lost:
You are the last one.

101

Miles accrued on an unknown road.
Questions: Welcome to brotherhood.
Surmised, but never certain.
Indoctrination and answers.
In time, in the myriad miracles,
An introductory course,
The lecture hall of life.
Years, decades, disappear.
National Sibling Day,
The first of many.
A road well-traveled, had we known.
Past the Hollywood sign,
Santa Barbara, Morro Bay.
Whittier, El Segundo, Atascadero.
Cities on the map,
California kings learning to drive.
When in the quiet twilight,
As the painted lanes blur,
We both realize.
We're lucky to be here.
Our classroom is within.
The atlas, unnecessary.
We know the terrain.
The pavement rises.
No signs, no accidents, no exits.
The highway was always there.

I HAVE THE NIGHT

In times of departure,
When our sun dips
Below the Pacific.
And the shadows grow
Long at LAX.
The calm creeps
Like lazy seagulls.
The orange horizon
Gives way to purple,
Then midnight blue,
Before the dark rules.
I ponder the destination.
Wonder as I wander,
Pilfering quiet moments
To myself, dreams in
Fluorescent light.
12 hours: Paradise.
I have the night.

A WINTER DAY IN WYOMING

Dead trees poke
Through the glazed white
Frosting, skeletons of
Snowmen never built.
The sky: majestic blue.
An azure hue beyond any view.
Rejoice in the frigid air.
You are alive, inhaling,
With snowshoes on your feet.
Old Faithful is faithfully yours.
You, hers. Embrace her heat.
Then you'll make love again.

I'M JUST AN ANT

I'm just an ant.
An insignificant stain
Overstepped by a
Benevolent alien.
A species so far
Advanced we can't
Communicate with them
And vice versa.

I'm just an ant.
I follow a long line
Of fellow ants,
Searching for a home
Free from extermination.
Our colony is vast.
But we don't pull
Our own weight.

I'm just an ant.
We strain to
Overcome the
Next hill. A beacon.
The pillagers.
And Earth is the
Garden we are
Infesting.

OVERWHELMING NUBILITY

I struggle for a definition.
Any answer, a key.
I saw you through an open door
Inside a dank bar on 14th Street.
On a damp night electrified by
Your patient gams, gems,
Baited beyond my control.
Pavlov's dogs' envy.
Black hair, beautiful hips,
Startling lips, eclipsed
All others under a drunken moon.
I had to dive in. Full.
Please pardon my swoon.

OBSTRUCTING ABSTRACTION

I can't think near your delicacy.
When you kill me with your body.
Imprison my thoughts with
Your willing hands. Unplanned.
Sing songs in perfect pitch.

Colors bend into a singularity.
The vision of you.
In my arms. And I in yours.
There is no confusion,
We are our own reunion.

Tapestries blend to infinity.
A stark scene leads to assuredness.
Contours mark your face.
I dream as you distract,
And we commit sensuous acts.

A NEW BEAST IN TOWN

They blew in on a train.
A couple destined for trouble.
Bonnie and Clyde reborn.
First stop, the bank:
To replenish their store.
Legal tender, taken legally.
All eyes stared.
Him with his baby blue suit.
Her with the green dress.
Arm in arm, striding tall.
They plunked money down
On the far side of town.
Dibs on a dilapidated hotel.
In time, a destination.
More beasts arrived.
All shuttered, naked,
In the gleaming gem.
Becoming new beasts.
Their pasts at their backs
As the old pair grinned.

HARD

A passion.
An engorged forge.
Arisen.
Louder.
Longitudinal.
Flaws and all.
Breaths prolonged.
Teeth clenched.
Sweat dripping
From the free flow
Of ideas, of bodies,
Of ecstatic curves.
Where are you?

FOSSILIZED HUMAN SKELETON FOUND ON MARS

Solis Lacus.
Lake for a day.
While the whole world waits,
While the dusty red sky
Consumes the horizon,
A monumental discovery.
An astronaut's nightmare
Broadcast for all.
A beacon. A demon.
Protruding from a
Blueberry grave.
First, a skeletal hand,
A marker to a wet past.
Clutches a black stone.
Hieroglyphics. Lyrics.
Lipograms and love.
The ghosts of Cairo.
The Earth visitor
Continues, digs deeper
Into expectant clay,
Revealing a fossilized
Human form:

Our past staring
At its future.
While back in the
Global living room:
Millions fall,
Entranced by dark snow.

SEA OF TOMORROW

I set out from the shore,
Seeking a horizon I
Will never meet,
A constant stripe,
Haunting, taunting.
Sometimes it's gray.
Others, blue or orange.
But permanent in its
Place on the earthly
Spectrum, the master.
I unfurl my sails.
The wind is that
Which I make,
That which I control.
My mast is my
Imagination, the rudder,
My undying dreams.
The sea will carry me.
The sea will be here,
With me: I forge on.

PREDILECTIONS

What would you have me do?
I am at your devious service.
Pray tell, cast your spell,
Evidence to the contrary
Is unwarranted.
I will love you in the sadness,
The darkness, the happiness,
The messiness of existence.
In fire, in cold, behold:
Your desires are my predilections.

ALONE IN A
DOWNTOWN HOTEL ROOM

Alone with my thoughts
In a downtown hotel room.
A sheet of gray penetrates
The view. Electric signs
Obscure my own
Intricate fantasies.
Wall Street shutters.
Bars close. 4:44 a.m.
A drunk cry pierces
The longing ether.
I am solo. TV snow
Reflects in the shadows.
Testing, one, two, three.
Life awaits this gentle hour.
A nubile companion will
Set me free, within
My mind's imagination.
You, a reality elsewhere,
We are the denizens
Of our own universe.
The rapture of your attention
Showers my incarnate chi.

As I marinate in truth:
The prospect of your body
Against mine powers eternity.
We'll never die.

SCAR

A line against time.
Engraved on my forehead,
Blood soaking the
L.A. Aztecs jersey.
Spatter, a memory.
Tissue rearranged.
A little brother's grip.
Pain and pressure.
Giant Tinkertoys,
Hidden away,
Flying through the air
While our parents
Pulled the handle on
The neon gods
In another desert.
We don't remember
Specific details.
Only laugh at the
Aftermath: a mark,
Of beautiful youth.
All hail the scar.

SUNRISE IN CANNES

Searching for decadence
On a cobblestone street.
The Mediterranean dream,
Night: a willing friend.
The stars, accomplices.
The limelight is off.
The Lumière lies still.
Dormant. The volcano
Awaits tomorrow's thrill,
When paparazzi pray.
Your thirst betrays you.
Aspirations flow,
Hunger pangs. Food, yes,
But something more.
A gleaming eye, a seductress.
Glances hover then pass.
And you find yourself
Eating salmon at 5 a.m.

WHEN EVERYONE HAS SEEN YOU NAKED

Birthday suits and Band-Aids.
What do you do when everyone
Has seen you naked?
Step by step and line by line.
Big, small, indifferent.
There isn't an alarm.
Your body, you're free.
Your amusement,
Hopefully, their glee.
Pause, rewind, stare.
The symptoms remain.
Remembered with care.
Curiosity and candlelight.
Nothing for the imagination.
Happily you waltz
Into the undiscussed fray.
Everyone is naked,
On every given day.

SPOTLIGHT

Your transient voice
Carries my desires
Into the wind.
Along the mantle
Of wistful hope.
Crushed fantasies
Hidden, defiled,
Stamped out.
Erased from the
Blackboard of hope.
I want your love cake.
No chance.
Not gonna happen.
I'm resigned to dream.
Tears welled
And suppressed.
My thoughts
Undressed:
Why would I put you
In the spotlight
When your need
Is cold as ice?

TEARS OF RAGE

I want to fuck around
And drive a Lamborghini.
Through Moroccan mountains.
Walk around in my underwear
On whitewashed Santorini
With an eager lover,
Dispatching care and inhibition.
Will the dirty socks matter
On your deathbed?
Unsettled dreams,
Unsettled minds,
Unsettled heartbreak.
Dishes piled high.
Green mountains cry
In the distance,
Echoing my desperate yell,
The anger within, unleashed,
Like discarded trash.
High and low, near and far.
The desert calls,
The desert wind my muse.
Namibia, Mongolia, Death Valley.
Without a penny in my name,
They remain in place,

Distant aspirations,
Feverish in their persistence.
Keen chance, a klaxon.
Can I just live?

WADING IN THE PLATTE

Somewhere near Kearney.
You are born dear.
The year: 1977. July.
Stepping stones unearthed.
You cannot drown:
A child's memory.
Under an infinite sky.
Dipped feet in summer's heat.
Water cold to the touch.
Budding lungs syncopated.
Wondering eyes dreaming
Of being old. Unfrozen.
This moment on a timeline.

I WISH

I wish I could make love to you.
Make you love to be loved,
Love to be made loved,
Made to be loved.
I wish I could see you naked.
Your brain and body open,
With all your scars.
With all your sins.
With your beauty marks
Marking me, like a shark.
I wish we gave each other
Hours of pleasure.
Unmeasured, legs in disarray.
Skin on skin, lips on lips.
Hands held tight
Drunk on our fluids.
I wish this weren't a dream.
Words made reality,
Realized in turn.
Are your clothes on the floor
Barely past the front door?
Alone, together,
In a dark room.
I wish.

URSA MAJOR

I saw you on a park bench,
Countenance contemplating
The nature of reality.
Mired in your own
Problems, your own world.
To each, they're overblown.
Fall leaves remained green.
Betraying Newton's
Inevitable plunge.
The midday sun hung tall.
Your eyes peeled to the sky.
An unopened book,
Burned the wood
By your side, beguiled.
I asked what was
More beautiful than
The pages of history,
The imagination bound
In a tome of artistic design.
You didn't blink, nor
Turn you head. Then
Squeezed my hand
Lightly, like a feather
From another galaxy,

And whispered:
"Let's not hibernate.
Tonight, we share the
Universe with Ursa Major."
And midnight never arrived.

BOLIVIA

You came here to get away
Yet everything is a mirror.
Salar de Uyuni.
Clouds upside down.
Chili powder, flamingoes,
Atacama visions.
By night, there is
No illusion.
The sky is an intrusion,
The ceiling with no name.
It's just an animal to tame.
I'm going to Bolivia.

You, reflected in the Milky Way.
Thoughts clear as glass.
Lost train cars train their
Inanimate thoughts
In a straight line.
Do you mind?
Awake unblind.
Follow the cirrus residue.
Climb the next frontier.
Sundance & Butch.
Leave your ghosts here.
I'm flying in Bolivia.

OCULUS

Long legs and heels,
Confused by the invasion
Of personal space
Beside a strange man.
Her aura outshines
All around her.
Blinding the walls,
And their secrets.
The parapets of the future.
The sounds of collusion.
Classic seduction.
A golden daisy
Who disappears into
The whiteness of
Architectural infinity.
A mother, holding a child,
Smiles, wanting, longing.
Thinking of her former days.
She sees the observer,
A distant star of desire.
Another man stops and leans
Into his other, plants a kiss.
Dreams of the past.
Dances back to the present.

The moment passes.
A son, tries on a shirt,
Wanting to be loved.
Wanting to reveal
His true eye, his true calling.
The watcher is watched.
Every eye is attuned.
Hoping to play a
Beautiful song, reading
Notes with the ease
Of Beethoven.
The opaque heaven recedes.
The ocular feast must end.

AVENUE X

She stands nude in a gateway.
A box of light etched on the floor,
A sunspot bound to Earth.
A cigarette dangles,
An extension of her right hand.
Eyes hidden as an elevated train
Rattles in the distance.
The tracks of her mind penetrate
The window, scream past pigeons,
Settle on a remembered door.
A past not taken, her red hair.
Curtains open on the top floor.
The Grande Dame of Avenue X.
6:00 a.m. Summer.
Gorgeous body, bountiful skin.
Thinking of Compartment C, Car 293.
Another train is her surreal destination.
She doesn't care who sees.

THE ETERNAL TERM PAPER

The test begins at birth,
You, totally unaware,
Dreaming of becoming old.
You learn to write, and words
Become fundamental tools,
Ways to process forever,
Immortal thoughts awaiting
A flaming fall into non-existence.
The teacher changes faces,
Places and techniques.
While you remain glued,
A perpetual pupil, graded,
Yesterday, today, tomorrow.
School is always in session.
Your vacation, not a digression.
Believe the cogent truth:
No matter how much you weigh,
You're always on the scale.

LETTER TO MY DESCENDANTS

If you are reading this,
And are my descendant,
Don't ascribe too much
Meaning into autobiography.
Or wallow in trying to
"Figure it out."
Discover the words
For yourself.
For the moments
You don't understand,
The moments you
Try to fill with
Unknowing meaning.
Maybe you can
Speak to my avatar:
In a sentient room.
That is one way.
Yet another is divine.
The DNA, the glitches
Passed on and examined.
Though we haven't met
Physically. Genetically,

Spiritually, willfully,
We are connected.
If you are perusing,
Devouring the words
And are not my descendant,
Are you not human too?
Do you still breathe with
Organic lungs? Bleed?
Perhaps your blood
Is synthetic and your
Exoskeleton leads
The peloton.
Somewhere in France
(If it exists).
We breathed air once.
I, a hoped ancestor,
Sending love forward.
How is the future
Atmosphere? An
Ocean of tears, but
For one simple fact:
We are *all* connected.

SUNCATCHER

Smiles in a tulip's blur.
Atmosphere unfurled:
Focus on the grin.
The way the hair shapes her face.
Your reciprocal simper.
Home in on the joy,
Emanating from the ether.
Spring. Yellow, white, red.
Life, a delicate flower,
Life, a vivacious little girl,
Laughing. Singing. Playing.
Running uphill.
There's infinite time still.
Before the planet tilts,
She lifts her head to the sky.
The suncatcher has my eye.

BEAUTY IN SUNLIGHT

I am a sequoia
In your presence.
Taller than all
The others.
A canopy for
Your dreams,
A lover for your
Lonely nights.
A bather for
Your shedding leaves.
I reach forever into
The sky, aloft atop
The rafters of delectation.
I am your sobriquet.
You wink, you grin,
We sin innate.
The dewy secretions
Of dawn signal
Our similar direction.
I am a disciple,
Thrusting higher.
Stridently, you are:
Beauty in sunlight.

HORRIBLE

Reprimanded,
Apologies demanded.
How can you find
Something
If you don't know
What you're
Looking for?
You're horrible,
You're horrible,
You're horrible.
Trifecta. Untied.
Sorry. If that's all
It took, would
There be
Anything lost
To begin with?
Calm yourself.
Heal. Accepted.
I atone. Gloze.
I meant you
No harm.
Let's not lose
Our charm.

LAND OF THE FREE

Free to yell "You Lie!".
Or punch a protestor.
Free to ignore the homeless.
Or laugh at it all.
Free to collude.
Or bathe in security.
Free to be complicit.
Or respect the Constitution.
Free to forgo health care.
Or get an education.
Free to gerrymander.
Or count chads.
Free to salute the flag.
Or "send them back".
Free to withstand reason
Or combat climate change.
Free to do as you please.
Or die as you say "I can't breathe".
Free to lie, cheat and steal.
Or capitalize on a free market.
Free to "Lock Her Up".
Or harbor racist thoughts.
Free to be a Republican.
Or a Democrat.

Free to be Independent.
Or legislate hate.
Free to realize, give a speech.
Or socialize, make peace.
Free to mass shoot a gun.
Or decide not to use one.
Free to form "a more perfect union".
Or worship, enraptured.
Free to be "free".
Or take necessary action.
Free to vote them out.
Or wallow in lactic acid.

THERE IS ONLY ONE CITY

There is only one city.
A bastion of glass and steel.
Never finished, ever rising.
We all have its state of mind.
One of a kind, in rhyme
Or metropolitan syncopation.
Empire built and bred.
Bakeries to bathhouses.
Milliners to millionaires.
Overwrought or undersold,
Nobody cares, taking dares.
Its heart beats in dreams,
Ashes of aspirations
Reclaimed by new arrivals,
Resold by old hands.
Taxis and talismans,
Share the gold streets.
Say it together, then repeat:
There is only one city.
We all live there.

REQUIEM FOR A STAR

The singing black hole
Begins this symphony,
While a little girl watches a hearse
Turn the corner of Hollywood and Vine.
First, she was a cloud of gas, pure, divine.
Developing ideas, readings, no sign of pain.
Then, a protostar: destined for luminance.
Taurus dreams, her winds rise, brisk.
Roles and hearts and seven figures,
A golden age, her main sequence.
Aged beauty, feelings swell, then become
A red giant, star on the Walk of Fame.
A walk of life, metal and heavier things.
A final explosion, Oscar,
The role of a lifetime.
Before the nebulae blow true. Convalesced.
It ends with a blue blast,
A permanent charade,
Dancing across the heavens.
Remnants of a white star or a void.
Stark contrast in the obituaries.
Missing black girl, missing white girl.
There is only one color, the color of our star.
No one is gone. No one shines brighter.
We're all stars here, we're all stars here.
Night sky: We all rest dear.

ANTHOLOGY OF PLEASURE

8:48 a.m.
Light filters through
A crack in undrawn blinds,
Seeking the denizens of this
Island paradise. A room, a ruse.
A taunting glimmer excites the
Aftermath of ecstatic passion.
Two lovers lost in dreams,
Their unclothed bodies curve
Into each other, a sensual
Möbius strip. Their thoughts
Align with the power of our regal star.
Another day of pressed flesh,
Of bikinis and bathing suits,
Pectoral muscles and cleavage.
Blood pumps, eyes converge.
There is no stopping it.
The carnival never ends.
Our mischievous duo awaits.

NUDITY, SEX, LOVE, BEAUTY

The disciples of Yayoi.
Late '60s free love.
Patronizing the
Patron saint of bliss.
Artists march on Fifth.

Ribald in their pageantry.
Nudity, sex, love, beauty.
The order of the procession,
Not necessarily a command.
Streaked clothes dyed.

As a plethora of polka dots
Rebel against the silent majority,
Institutionalized conformity.
Paint the world; erase dark clouds.
Your body, bare, is at the door.

WORLD 4

There is no 1, 2 or 3.
There is only World 4.
Not a war. A destination.
A unified planet.
One nation under Logic,
Logos and Love.
Free to worship
As you will without
Legislating the Body.
Peace is supreme.
Common sense:
The abundant currency.
Hedonism, if you will.
The spinning globe
Spans division.
While Mercury descends.

DESIDERATUM

What do you desire?
The barest of essentials:
You and your completion.
Given in trust and tryst.
Eager to energize,
Eager to cure.
The curves, the sighs,
The transmuted emotions.
Happiness is my body,
Inclined to you.
Performing great feats
With vigorous sex appeal.
Twins in captured thought.
I transform in your corona.
I need nothing else.

ALL THE PRETTY PEOPLE

There's no need
For velvet ropes.
The democracy
Of resplendency
Rules this itinerant city.
We're all beautiful.
We're all cool.
Cold in the sense
Of all things go,
The golden trope
Of do me like you do you.
Everyone has a
Spectacular angle.
Freedom is the docent.
Lost in the shadows
Of skyscrapers,
Let perfection rain:
All the pretty people.
No one's ugly here.

9°

How long has it been?
The fresh scent of love,
Withering in the throes
Of a brutal cold spell.
Lenticular clouds, immobile,
Obscure the joyful sun.
A walk across the
Brooklyn Bridge,
Ice-filled, desires chilled,
Etches scars in my
Dopamine receptors.
Photographs reveal only
The outer landscape,
The laughs and cries
Remain hidden, mindful
Of their cerebral prison.
My breath streaks like acid
Into the crystal blue sky.
When I realize, a snowy dagger:
Winter is inside me.

WONG KAR WAI

He loves us for 10,000 years.
Sound designed by hope,
Edited by poetry and
Lensed by vivid reveries.
Etched in the senses
Like a pierced heart
In romantic seas.
How much energy will the
Sun shed in this span?
How much love is lost?
Entropy of the Gods.
In the mood beyond 2046.
The sanguine heart of
Infinite stars, wondrous
Trains, side by side,
Forever combined,
Destiny intertwined:
Celluloid eternity.
Critics speak into
An unknown hole.
Because his secrets
Enchant us still.

TRIBE HUMAN

Tribe Human: origin,
A term for every stripe
For people of every type.
We unite, we defy hate.
One planet, alone,
One common home.
Clothed in compassion.
Washed in unanimous
Concern for one another.
The blood we share,
The love we make.
The hats we wear.
Become one of many.
Welcome to your tribe.

THE AURA OF YOUR DREAMS

You are a stark lamp
On the street of unpaved
Imagination, a monument
Through ordained dust and
Waning sunlight. Bright.
The guide of Dreamland.
I forge my salient way
Beyond reaching darkness,
Through the infinite forest
Of unending thoughts that
Proceed in this twilight,
Like when we drowned in
The majesty of Tottori dunes
Beneath a silver sky
Filled with forever.
With you, my consort,
I too am a lamp.
We blend into one beam,
Where I bask in the
Aura of your dreams.

THE PLANET WE LIVE ON

I.

You are here. I am here. We are here.
Where dinosaurs frolicked,
And their bones remain,
Licking the laptop of sin.
This is our planet.
This is our world.
Crime and punishment drawn
Like a magnet, pungent grins.
People born, people expired.
The planet still spins.

II.

The Amazon burns.
The sea belches plastic.
Politicians grab pussies.
Guns, guns, guns.
Abolish the Electoral College.
Frequent visitors to the men's room
Legislate women's bodies.
End the charade. Blue sea,
Blue you. Blue hue.
Hindsight is 2020.

III.

The highest peaks bear the streaks,
The marks of explorers, bustling feats.
Sands worn by time whistle songs.
Parks need to be designated.
But even then, bled dry.
Wind, heat, global change.
The drumbeat continues.
The rhythm doesn't rearrange.
We are the architects.
The governors of shame.

IV.

Continents and countries.
My world is filled by
Things that divide.
Borders and binders.
Don't exist on the Earth.
On the dirt beneath our feet.
Illusions, they lurk in the mind,
Waiting to lash out.
Waiting to be unkind.
Walls will not save us.

V.

Norway, France, Spain,
Portugal, England, Germany.
Italy, Russia, Iceland.
Switzerland, Belgium,
The Netherlands.
Puzzle pieces of travel.
European parcels.
Places I've been.
When the sphere is gone,
Names will be too.

VI.

Japan, China, Thailand.
The eyes of Fujiyama.
The lanterns of Gifu,
The beaches of Iwo Jima.
Tiananmen Square, Hong Kong.
Revolts of geography: a solution.
Australia, New Zealand,
Far afield in Oceania,
Let's dream of one peace.

VII.

Six hundred and sixty-six ways.
America, where is your place?
Novus Ordo Seclorem.
Control, Mexico won't pay.
Canada will heal your wounds.
South America, the lungs, the
Liquid we need. Brazil:
Minerals and feed the world.
Indigenous dreams from Pachacamac.
As we dance on the Ecuadorian equator.

VIII.

The poles, a litmus test for Terra Firma.
The midst of the Great Extinction.
Sunset tinctures illuminate the carnage.
Polar bears fade, Arctic terns cry.
While ice fishers float by.
Where is the soil? Where is the hand?
No composure, no grace, no kludge.
Hearts may listen, skip in place.
Chemicals cleaning or boiling?
Let's hear the klaxon of the ages.

IX.

Little girls lie in bed.
Sleeping, dreaming, breathing.
Their hair furls together in
Matching pajamas. Angels
Deciding our future.
Awake, awake.
A planetary wake.
Fill the parks with the
Laughter of children,
Their purity and their questions.

X.

Stilt fishers in Sri Lanka
Ply their trade above damaged shores.
Their happiness, infectious.
Their hopes, triumphant.
They will catch the biggest fish.
They will achieve the impossible.
Unblinded minds unbowed by tsunami.
They are the maelstrom.
They are the fire of accomplishment.
Smile among them and learn.

XI.

The keys of tomorrow
Revel in zeros and ones.
Machines, quantum, molecular,
Magistrations of immense power.
See the galaxies. See the moon.
Look for a new home to ruin.
Or a new home to cherish?
Latter stages of regret are best
Fixed in the present.
Nanotechnology can be a friend.

XII.

Grains and gravels.
Saharan sojourn.
Salmon grown beyond.
Urban farms rescuing
The human plight.
We indulge in restitution
While a new slight arises.
From Mt. Everest to the
Dead Sea. Finite resources,
Infinite possibilities.

XIII.

Batman and Robin.
Comic book heaven.
The pleasant urges of
Human imagination.
Seek a solution, a prayer.
Allay any requiem.
Erase all destruction.
The trees will tell the tale.
Tall and bold. Redwood bliss,
Climbing toward eternity.

XIV.

A contention of species,
Their mark on our home.
Sentient whales seek
A clean deep: Neptune's Bellows.
From Antarctica to Alaska.
Snow used to fall. Ice used
To carve landscapes, red, erect.
What evidence will you leave?
Stained gadgets, dead mice,
Rusted steel. Fleeting states.

XV.

Seven billion plus and counting.
There is no neon countdown,
No advertising jingle.
The curators adjudicate laws,
Placing man's hand over nature.
Courtrooms. Reality TV, manure.
They fertilize and engender rows.
Celebrities sell products,
Baking fantasy, a willing distraction.
Lights, camera factions.

XVI.

A blue dot in the void.
A smear in the blink of time.
Stars come and go,
Other worlds rejoice, belch,
Extract glimpses through a lens.
Scientists glance. Governments fall.
Rebels fill the vacuum,
Their mantras echo to Mars.
Oceans and skies. We realize
They are our friends.

XVII.

Wadi Rum awaits my call,
Its vistas eroding as I write.
Science fiction, Petra.
The ghosts of Harrison.
Beyond the horizon.
One point on a spinning top.
Artists, mathematicians.
From Persia to Jerusalem.
Jewels of human endeavor.
Will it persist, wayfarers and all?

XVIII.

Beethoven, Mahler, Chopin.
Lyrical mythos never digested.
The notes remain in the firmament.
Beamed on lasers, bonded screams.
Heralding gold, frankincense, myrrh.
Under a cataclysmic luminescence.
Latitude unknown. Games give rise
To Herculean heights. Men, women,
Atop the podium of riches.
Everyone is an Olympian.

XIX.

From Greece to Egypt,
Rome to France. Guggenheim
And the Louvre oeuvre.
Magritte lifts the clouds,
Predicts the endless reverie,
Museums built, expanded,
Looted, withstood.
The first women huddled
By fire in a cave, drawing
Modeled men. Staving war.

XX.

Geographic diversity.
Biological mercy.
The Pyramids of Giza,
Rainforests, Mauna Kea,
Stromboli, California,
Where celluloid warps,
Bends and enlightens,
All at the same—the sane—time.
We believe what we want to.
Every landscape under the sun.

XXI.

There is hope in the madness.
In the ever tilting renaissance
Of the collective unconscious.
A word. An idea. A revolution.
Love, the unbridled pacifier,
Waiting for hordes of babies.
Unapologetic, hectic, electric.
Missiles silenced, hateful banter
Quenched. Reside in the better aura,
The tectonic sex of preservation.

XXII.

The planet I live on has beauty,
Falcons, flowers, fauna,
High-minded infidels we conquer fear.
I stand atop Dune 7, slide down
A topography of polyamory,
Embrace my enemy.
We don't have much time.
We make love and live.
We create: a "perfect" union.
The planet we live on is still.

EPILOGUE:
I/XXI

Roman porno.
Roman calendar.
Roman numerals.
When In Rome,
Do as the Romans do?
Agree or disagree.
Live around the fragments.
Of time. Of temerity.
Sing and play your chords.
They will linger longer
Than Elysian Fields.
I'll sleep when I'm read.

ACKNOWLEDGMENTS

Most importantly, I thank my family. I am also deeply grateful for all of my friends in NYC and around the world. Thank you to anyone who has ever written, read or listened to a poem, and to those of you who are thinking about it. I believe the definition of poetry is subjective. It can be a single word, or a 50,000 line epic tale of free verse, or a painting, a glance, a film, a photograph, a sculpture, an amazing design, a play, a lover, a glass of milk or the glint in your children's eyes. Poetry is life and vice versa. I hope you enjoy this latest collection. Thank you: the reader, the watcher, the seeker, the human being.

OTHER WORK BY KELVIN C. BIAS

MILKMAN (Novel)

What happens when everyman Calder Boyd starts to lactate? The Manhattanite becomes a media cause célèbre nicknamed the Milkman and old and new problems spill forth. The son of a former NBA star and a Norwegian artist, Calder copes with his strained marriage, losing his copywriting job at a boutique ad agency, a male-empowerment espousing mailman and a porn-star performance artist who wants to exploit him. He also deals with his late father's legacy and his wife's past indiscretion—all while breastfeeding their newborn daughter. Calder eventually becomes a pawn in the battle between a feminist organization and a militant men's society as he tries to become a better husband and man. The Fourth Estate, sex, art, love, memory, marriage and family converge during the snowiest winter on record in this commentary on contemporary American fatherhood.

WHISPERS OF A DYING SUN (Poetry)

These poems represent the vestiges of man from the perspective of a distant future. Akin to radio signals, the remnants of humanity streak toward a black hole where art, politics, love, technology, philosophy, science and the yearning for eternity accrete. Prophetic, stoic, polyphasic, the words disassemble and recombine on the other side in search of a new sun. I hope these poems find a closer home in your personal universe, heard but you're unsure of their origin, like whispers.

SEXOPOLIS: POEMS ON LOVE AND SEX

Love is a liberation, an act, a rebellion, a restriction, a communion. This poetry collection covers the universal topics of love and sex. From erotic to platonic and from marital to familial, love comes in many forms. We don't always get it, but we all crave it.

IMMACULATE DUST: LOVE POEMS

This poetry collection delves headlong into the world of love. Encompassing the realms of dream, fantasy and reality, the poems intend to engender not just love, but more pointedly, lovemaking. Lust. Love. Languor. These are three states of mind and body before, during and after the most pleasant poetry of human interaction: consented sex. We all possess desire and we are all made of dust. Immaculate dust.

ABOUT THE AUTHOR

Kelvin C. Bias is a journalist, novelist, poet, filmmaker, raconteur and aesthete. However, his most important moniker is father. He lives in Brooklyn with his wife and daughters.

21 Particles of Eternity is his fourth poetry collection. Connect with Kelvin on Instagram & Twitter: @archivezero

www.ingramcontent.com/pod-product-compliance
Lightning Source LLC
LaVergne TN
LVHW051413080426
835508LV00022B/3061